EVERYTHING
VIKINGS

NATIONAL GEOGRAPHIC KiDS

EVERYTHING VIKINGS

NADIA HIGGINS

With Vikings Expert ANDREW JENNINGS

NATIONAL GEOGRAPHIC
WASHINGTON, D.C.

CONTENTS

Men and boys dressed in Viking garb prepare to celebrate the annual Up Helly Aa midwinter fire festival on the Shetland Islands in Scotland.

Vikings didn't wait to be invited. They attacked villages, ransacking them for treasure.

INTRODUCTION

"RUTHLESS, WARLIKE, SAVAGE, BRUTAL ... " ENGLISH WRITERS COULDN'T FIND

harsh enough words to describe them. Those pirates who charged from strange boats. Who plundered houses and kidnapped women. Who stabbed men in their beds. Vikings!

For 250 years, Vikings struck fear into the hearts of the people of medieval Europe—and with good reason. Vikings were Norse, or Scandinavian, warriors who looted or conquered parts of England, France, Germany, Ireland, Italy, Russia, Scotland, and Spain. But that's just one part of the story.

The Vikings were also traders. They founded cities and opened trade routes connecting far-flung corners of the world. They were bold explorers who set foot in North America 500 years before Christopher Columbus. The Vikings were known for their poetry and mythology, as well as for their magnificent sailing ships and beautiful jewelry. And during a time when other women had little control over their own lives, Viking women were surprisingly powerful.

The Vikings changed the face of medieval Europe. Even today, almost a thousand years after the peak of their power, they still loom large in our imaginations. So put on your helmet and grab your shield. Let's find out EVERYTHING about Vikings.

EXPLORER'S CORNER

Hi! I'm Dr. Andrew Jennings, and I'm a historian. For the last 20 years, I have been learning as much about the Vikings as possible and trying to discover new, unknown things about these amazing people. I find them so interesting that, for nearly ten years now, I have been living in Shetland where the Vikings settled more than a thousand years ago. When you start your Viking expedition, look for me in the Explorer's Corner. I'll share my knowledge of Viking history, traditions, culture, and other cool stuff!

MEET THE VIKINGS

Vikings were skilled seafarers and warriors who risked dangerous sea crossings and battles to claim riches, and later, land to live on.

WHO WERE THE VIKINGS?

IMAGINE IF YOU REALLY COULD MEET

A VIKING. YOU'VE GONE BACK TO THE VIKING AGE, BETWEEN
A.D. 793 and 1066. Standing in front of you is a bearded man in a leather helmet. He is a Viking, and he is speaking Old Norse. He comes from Scandinavia, and his home is a patchwork of rival kingdoms, which we know today as Denmark, Norway, and Sweden. Like many Vikings, he is a gifted storyteller. He'll tell you how his people developed the world's most advanced ships. They have sailed as far west as North America, south to Africa, and east into Russia's rivers. What do they seek? Fortune of all kinds. They're most famous for raiding monasteries and towns. But they conquer and settle land as well, and they are clever traders. Back home, the Viking's family members earn their livelihood as farmers, fishers, and craftspeople.

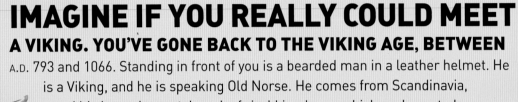

Vikings in longships on a raiding expedition head toward the coast of England.

NORSE NOTE THE WORD "VIKING" WAS FIRST USED IN ENGLISH IN 1801.

Viking raiders attack monks at an Irish monastery.

WHAT'S IN A NAME?

A thousand years ago, nobody used the word "Viking." When they saw Norse ships approaching their shores, English peasants probably yelled something like, "The Northmen are coming!" In Old Norse, *vikingr* meant something along the lines of pirate. Technically, Vikings are only those who took to the sea, but most historians use the word for the whole culture, just for convenience. The vast majority of Scandinavian farmers of that time would be puzzled to know we call them Vikings today.

TELLING TALES

The Vikings didn't leave much of a written record. So, how do we know so much about them?

SAGAS

Starting in the 12th century, when the Viking age was over, Scandinavian poets who were descendants of the Vikings began writing down the stories Vikings had passed down orally, from person to person, for generations. These stories, about famous battles, fantastic heroes and heroines, and legendary voyages, were called *sagas*, which is the Old Norse word for "story."

DIGS

Archaeologists try to match the history told in the sagas with the human bones, bits of pottery, jewelry, and coins they find in burial mounds, villages, and treasure troves. These buried objects are found in areas of the world where Vikings are known to have raided, traded, or lived.

OUTSIDER ACCOUNTS

The writings of Irish monks and Arab traders give a glimpse of how other people viewed the Vikings. These handwritten manuscripts often did not paint a flattering picture.

RUNES

Runes are letters of the old Scandinavian alphabet. Runic inscriptions are short messages carved onto wood, metal, and stone. Runic inscriptions are found throughout Europe on jewelry, weapons, and even on walls and stones in areas settled by the Vikings. Runic writing sometimes marks graves, or lists charms, spells, or even laws.

By the Numbers

5 TONS of animal bones, left over from medieval meals, were excavated from the Viking town in York, England.

30 men could sail in a Viking knarr, or cargo ship, which was wider than a longship and was used to haul trade goods.

350 Viking ships—in probably the largest Viking fleet ever—raided London in A.D. 851.

617 silver coins, plus 65 pieces of silver and gold jewelry, and other items from a mid-tenth-century Viking hoard, were found by amateur treasure hunters in North Yorkshire, England, in 2007.

960 years after it was abandoned, archaeologists found remnants of a Viking settlement in North America, at L'Anse aux Meadows, Newfoundland, Canada.

TRADERS AND RAIDERS

WHAT DO YOU DO IN SCANDINAVIA IN A.D. 800, WHEN

farmland is scarce, and the population is booming? You just might join a raiding party to Ireland or England. An expedition across the sea promised wealth and glory. Vikings in Scandinavia lived on islands and peninsulas that were surrounded by sea so they became expert sailors and shipbuilders. Vikings undertook four main types of seafaring expeditions: trading, raiding, conquering, and exploring. But the lines between one type of voyage and another were often blurred.

TRAVELING TRADERS

Even before the Viking age, Scandinavians were selling their wares, such as honey, wool, and fish, in foreign markets. As time went on, their vast trading networks stretched from Greenland all the way east into central Asia. There were no easy routes between these parts of the world. Traders spent months or years trudging across dangerous or difficult territory. Swedish traders founded routes as far east as Constantinople (now Istanbul) and Jerusalem.

VIKING TIME LINE

793	841	865	870	882
• The Viking age kicks off with a surprise attack on the monastery of Lindisfarne—an island off the coast of England.	• Norwegian Vikings establish Dublin, Ireland, as a winter base. It became a major Viking trading city.	• Danish Vikings invade England. Eventually, over many decades, they settle the eastern half of England.	• Norwegian Vikings begin migrating to Iceland.	• Kiev, in present-day Ukraine, becomes a Swedish stronghold and trading center.

Viking loot included gold, silver, and jewels.

RAID, THEN CONQUER!

Early on, raids were short summer events. The first recorded Viking raid happened in A.D. 793 off the east coast of England. Summer raids took place after spring planting in Scandinavia. A Viking fleet of two to ten longships would head to the shores of Ireland and the British Isles. Their longships glided right onto the beach. Then the raiders would snatch as much as they could and dash back to the boat. As the Viking age went on, raiding parties became bigger. Raiders spent the winter in their raiding lands. Grabbing loot was no longer enough—the Vikings thirsted for land. Armed with swords and axes, they battled the armies of the lands they wanted to conquer. The victorious Vikings then settled in their captured lands.

FIND NEW TERRITORY

Sometimes, Viking ships landed in new territory after being blown off course during storms. Tales of the new lands would spread through word of mouth. With these tales in mind, other Vikings sailed west into the uncharted waters of the North Atlantic. These daring explorers sought new land. Vikings traveled to Iceland, Greenland, and the northeastern shore of North America. Iceland and Greenland became successful settlements, while a North American settlement was abandoned, perhaps because it was so far from their homeland, or because of clashes with native North Americans.

ERIK THE RED

A VIKING WHO, WHAT, WHERE

Viking, Norse, Nordic, Norway—there are a lot of different names, terms, and countries mentioned in Viking history. Some of the places Vikings came from weren't yet countries as we know them now. Here's a useful list of the terms for Viking language, people, and places.

VIKING

Describes the seafaring Scandinavian people and culture from the Viking age (A.D. 793 to 1066).

SCANDINAVIA

Scandinavia is a geographic term used to describe the area of northern Europe that includes the modern countries of Denmark, Norway, and Sweden.

VIKING PEOPLE

Norwegians come from Norway, Danes come from Denmark, and Swedes come from—you guessed it—Sweden. All of these people were part of the Viking culture.

OLD NORSE LANGUAGE

The Vikings spoke a language we call Old Norse. The terms Norse and Nordic also refer to Viking people and culture.

911	c. 986	c. 1000	1016	1050s
• Viking leader Rollo gains control of Normandy, in present-day France.	• Erik the Red leads a party of Icelanders to settle in Greenland.	• Leif Eriksson leads an expedition to the northeastern coast of North America.	• Cnut the Great begins rule over a Viking empire that covers Denmark, England, and Norway.	• Denmark, Norway, and Sweden become three separate kingdoms.

FAMOUS VIKING FEATS

VIKINGS ENTERTAINED EACH OTHER BY TELLING STORIES AND RECITING POEMS

about their most jaw-dropping feats. If Vikings were still alive today, what tales would they be telling around the fire? Here are just a few of the Viking feats that still baffle and amaze us.

VARANGIAN GUARD

SLY SWINDLERS

Perhaps nobody feared the Vikings more than Ethelred the Unready, England's king from A.D. 978 to A.D. 1016. During his reign, Ethelred started making regular payments to Danish chiefs just for *not* attacking England. This forced payment, or extortion, has its own Viking name—Danegeld. By 1012, Ethelred had paid out a whopping 48,000 pounds (21,800 kg) of silver in total.

ETHELRED THE UNREADY

BADDEST BODYGUARDS

In A.D. 988, Basil II, emperor of the Byzantine Empire, was fed up with his own disloyal guards. So, he offered the job to Vikings. Basil lured Scandinavia's best and bravest with promises of gold. This elite unit was called the Varangian Guard. To apply, a Viking man had to undertake a yearlong trip to Constantinople. Then he had to prove his skills in ordinary combat. Big muscles and a menacing air were also important.

NORSE NOTE THE VIKINGS LOVED SKIING AND EVEN WORSHIPPED A SKIING GOD NAMED ULLR.

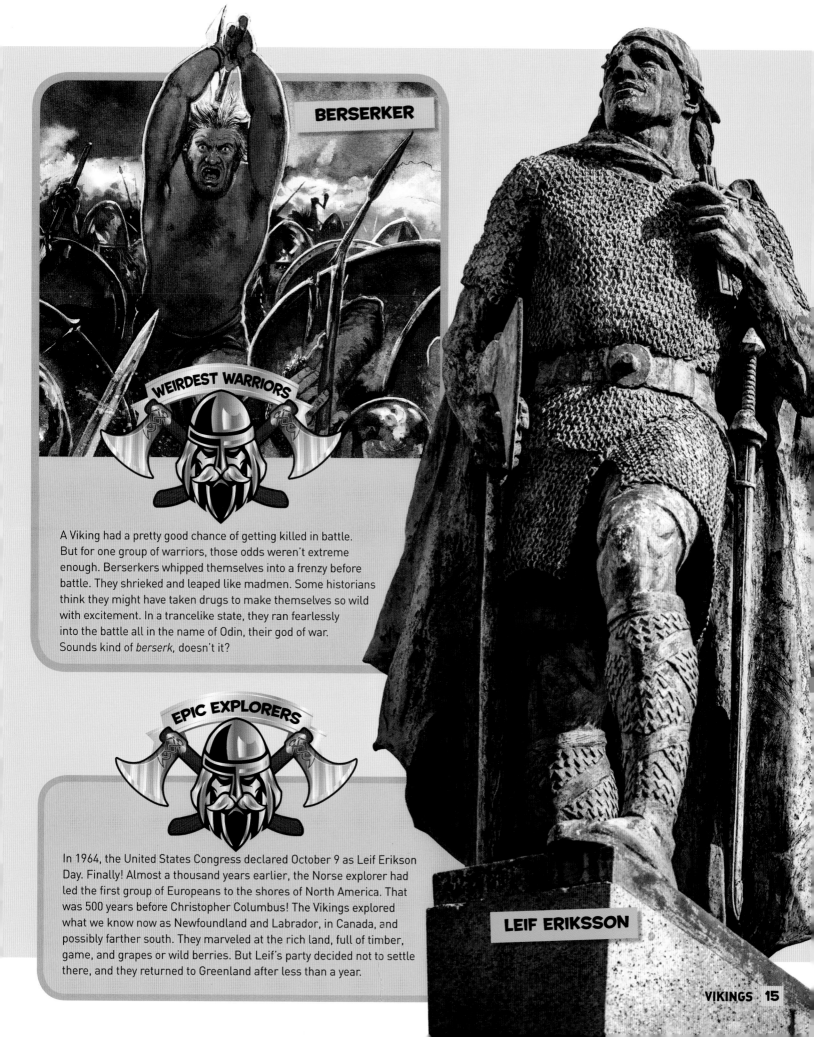

BERSERKER

WEIRDEST WARRIORS

A Viking had a pretty good chance of getting killed in battle. But for one group of warriors, those odds weren't extreme enough. Berserkers whipped themselves into a frenzy before battle. They shrieked and leaped like madmen. Some historians think they might have taken drugs to make themselves so wild with excitement. In a trancelike state, they ran fearlessly into the battle all in the name of Odin, their god of war. Sounds kind of *berserk*, doesn't it?

EPIC EXPLORERS

In 1964, the United States Congress declared October 9 as Leif Erikson Day. Finally! Almost a thousand years earlier, the Norse explorer had led the first group of Europeans to the shores of North America. That was 500 years before Christopher Columbus! The Vikings explored what we know now as Newfoundland and Labrador, in Canada, and possibly farther south. They marveled at the rich land, full of timber, game, and grapes or wild berries. But Leif's party decided not to settle there, and they returned to Greenland after less than a year.

LEIF ERIKSSON

THE VIKING WORLD

NEWFOUNDLAND

In 1960, archaeologists unearthed the Viking camp at L'Anse aux Meadows in Newfoundland, Canada. The discovery proved that Vikings had explored North America and established, for a time, the earliest known European settlement on the continent.

BY 1001, HARDLY ANY
PART OF EUROPE REMAINED UNTOUCHED

by Viking conquest, trade, or exploration. The Vikings spread out in three main directions. Norwegians sailed west to Ireland and Scotland, then on through the North Atlantic. The Danes ventured south into England and France. The Swedes headed east into Russia.

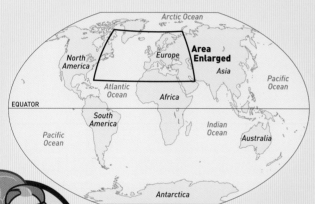

Map labels: Arctic Ocean · North America · Europe · **Area Enlarged** · Asia · Atlantic Ocean · Africa · Pacific Ocean · EQUATOR · South America · Indian Ocean · Australia · Pacific Ocean · Antarctica

Map labels (right): GREENLAND · NORTH AMERICA · CANADA · Atlantic Ocean · L'Anse aux Meadows · Newfoundland

EXPLORER'S CORNER

In the British Isles, place-names tell us where the Vikings settled. The Norwegian Vikings settled in Shetland, Orkney, northern Scotland, the Hebrides, the Isle of Man, and Cumbria. They have left us the names of their farms such as Gremista, after a Viking called Grimr, and the names of islands, bays, and mountains. The Danish Vikings settled mainly in England. They have left us names such as Scarborough, the fort of a Viking warrior called Skarthi.

L'ANSE AUX MEADOWS

NORSE NOTE THE VIKING VILLAGE AT L'ANSE AUX MEADOWS, NEWFOUNDLAND, WAS ONLY UNCOVERED IN 1960.

IRELAND

By the A.D. 820s, Vikings were raiding Ireland from all sides. Irish monasteries were a favorite Viking target. Vikings eventually established settlements in Ireland, including the Kingdom of Dublin. Over time, the Vikings married into Irish families and the two cultures were blended.

HOMELAND

Travel through Scandinavia's mountains and forests wasn't easy. Plus, islands, fjords, and bays offered miles of winding coastline. It's no wonder Vikings took to ships!

ICELAND

Norwegian Vikings settled Iceland starting in A.D. 870. It became a thriving Viking colony. Iceland's deep Viking roots are shown in its language. Modern Icelandic is remarkably similar to Old Norse. Most Icelanders can read the sagas written almost a thousand years ago.

RUSSIA AND UKRAINE

Swedish Vikings dragged their boats over land and into rivers to sail through modern-day Russia and Ukraine. Under Swedish rule, Kiev, in modern Ukraine, and Novgorod, in Russia, became bustling trade centers.

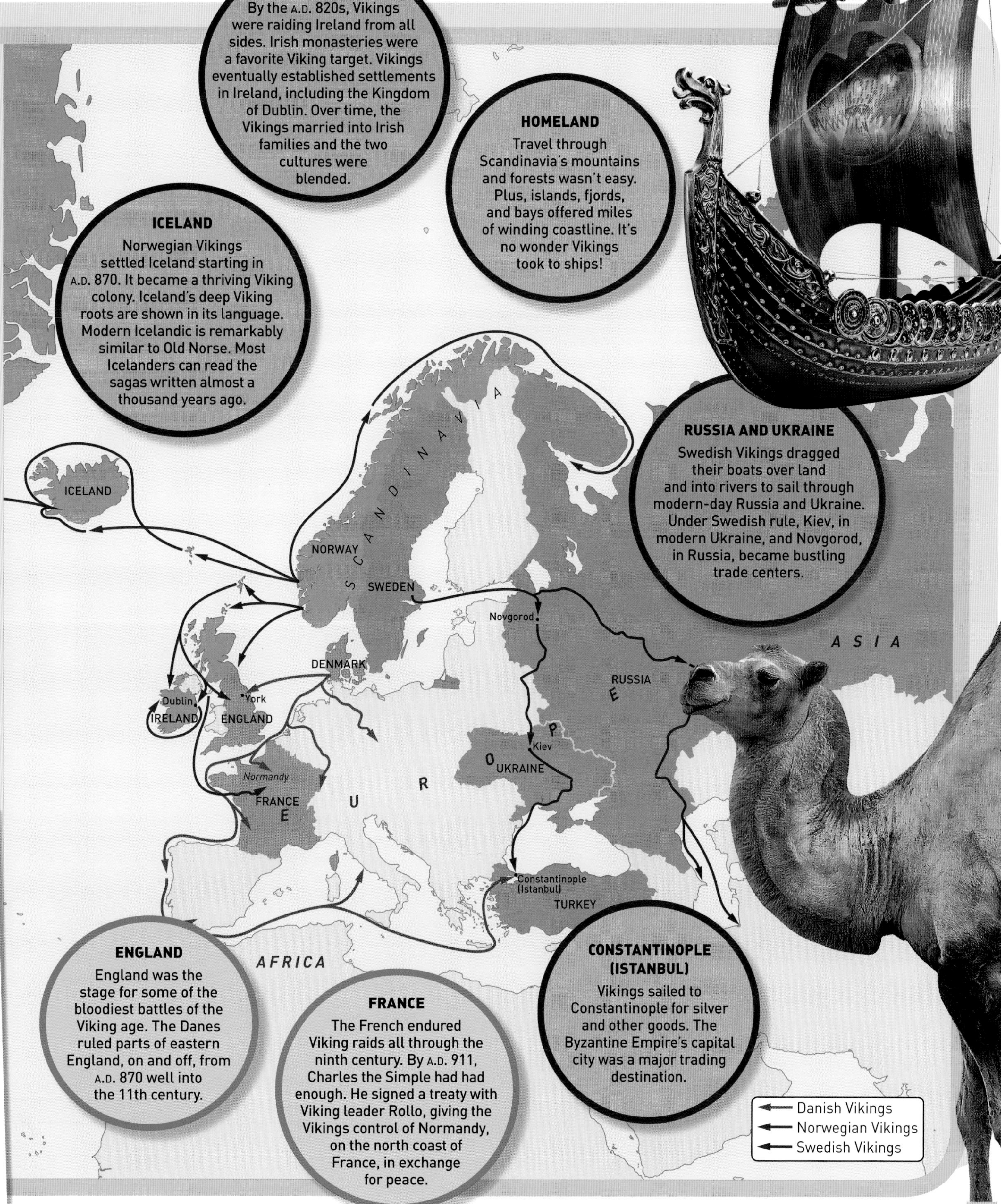

SCANDINAVIA
ICELAND
NORWAY
SWEDEN
DENMARK
Novgorod
ASIA
RUSSIA
EUROPE
Dublin
York
IRELAND
ENGLAND
Kiev
UKRAINE
Normandy
FRANCE
Constantinople (Istanbul)
TURKEY
AFRICA
Danish Vikings
Norwegian Vikings
Swedish Vikings

ENGLAND

England was the stage for some of the bloodiest battles of the Viking age. The Danes ruled parts of eastern England, on and off, from A.D. 870 well into the 11th century.

FRANCE

The French endured Viking raids all through the ninth century. By A.D. 911, Charles the Simple had had enough. He signed a treaty with Viking leader Rollo, giving the Vikings control of Normandy, on the north coast of France, in exchange for peace.

CONSTANTINOPLE (ISTANBUL)

Vikings sailed to Constantinople for silver and other goods. The Byzantine Empire's capital city was a major trading destination.

AN ILLUSTRATED DIAGRAM

VIKING LONGSHIP

FORGET COMFORT OR CARGO

SPACE. A VIKING LONGSHIP WAS DESIGNED FOR two main advantages: speed and agility. This warship skimmed ocean waves, but it could also be rowed up a river. Unlike other ships of the day, it could glide right up to a beach. Vikings stormed ashore before the locals knew what hit them.

RAISE THE MAST!
The mast was raised for sailing but lowered for rowing.

65 TO 95 FEET (20 TO 29 M) LONG

40 TO 80 OARSMEN

SHIELD RACK
Warriors hung their shields on the outside of the boat to protect the boat from wind and waves, and to keep them out of the way when the men were walking on the ship.

15 TO 30 PAIRS OF OARS

DRAGON HEAD

A fearsome carving of a snake, dragon, or other beast on the front, or prow, of a ship was meant to scare off hostile sea monsters. It may have been removed when landing, however, so as not to upset land sprites.

SQUARE SAIL

Brightly colored sails struck fear in the hearts of onlookers. The colorful cloth doubled as a roof when a storm blew in. Viking ships also had oars for rowing when the wind was not blowing, or to move down rivers when they needed to move fast.

FOR SEA AND RIVERS

The boat's body, or hull, was shallow enough to ride on rivers and under bridges.

17 FEET (5 M) WIDE

STEERING STRAIGHT

A single piece of wood formed the boat's "spine," or keel. This innovation reduced rolling from side to side, increasing speed. It also made steering easier.

WHICH WAY, CAPTAIN?

A Viking captain's number one rule? Keep land in sight whenever possible. Otherwise, Viking sailors studied stars, waves, seabirds, and the color of ocean water to find their way. By the late tenth century, they had figured out how to use the sun's position to measure their progress north and south.

Sunstones are natural crystals that change color in the sun. They allowed Viking sailors to determine the sun's position even on a cloudy day.

SUNSTONE

In Viking mythology, Valkyries swooped down from the sky on horses to claim men killed in battle and bring them to Valhalla, the Viking hall of the slain.

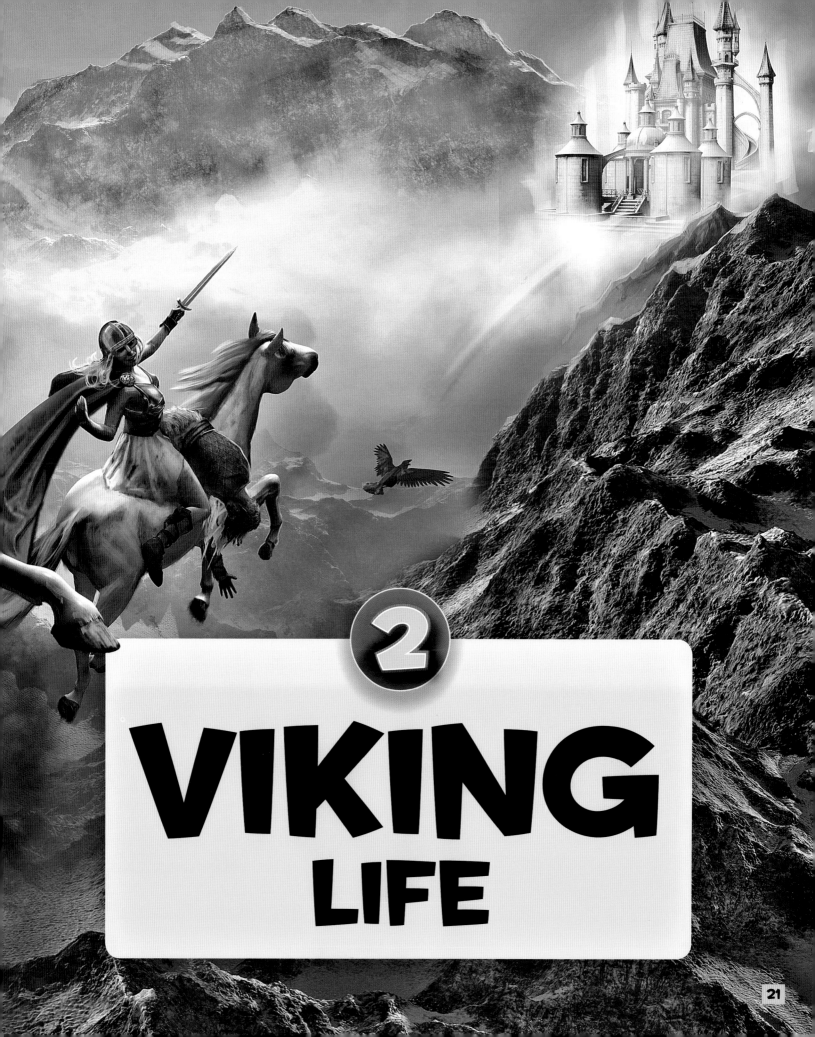

2

VIKING
LIFE

JARLS, KARLS, AND THRALLS

VIKING KING

VIKINGS DEFINITELY
KNEW THEIR PLACE IN SOCIETY.

At the top were the kings, followed by jarls, then karls, then thralls. But class structure wasn't as rigid as it was elsewhere in Europe. Even a regular farmer could improve his social standing by racking up riches on raids abroad.

BOLD AND BRAVE

Vikings valued personal honor, bravery, and self-control. Showing weakness or going back on your word caused great disgrace that extended to your entire family. Revenge killings were a basic right. These beliefs were made into laws, and everyone—even kings—had to obey them.

AT A **VIKING FEAST,** EVERYONE SAT IN AN **ASSIGNED SEAT** ACCORDING TO **STATUS,** WITH **THRALLS** SEATED **FARTHEST** FROM **KINGS AND JARLS.**

TOP DOG

Viking society was composed of many small kingdoms. Some kings ruled over small territories that included several villages. Others, such as Cnut the Great, king of Denmark, England, Norway, and parts of Sweden from A.D. 1016 to 1035, conquered and ruled vast territories. A king was always looking over his shoulder. Any member of the royal family could vie for his seat. Neighboring kings posed a constant threat. As one king cleverly put it, "A king is for glory, not for long life."

NORSE NOTE A GOOD HORSE WAS A STATUS SYMBOL IN VIKING CULTURE, LIKE A FANCY CAR IS TODAY.

JARL

SECOND-IN-COMMAND

A jarl, or nobleman, could rival a Viking king in power, though technically he was of lower rank. A good jarl impressed his subjects with generous gifts and lavish feasts. So when it came time to go on a raid, they would gladly follow him.

KARL

ORDINARY OLAFS

Mostly, a karl was a farmer or a fisherman, but merchants, craftsmen, and traders fell into this group as well. Karls followed jarls and kings on raids, so long as they could afford their own weapons.

THRALL

BOTTOM OF THE HEAP

A thrall was a slave, either born into captivity or kidnapped in battle. Most thralls were laborers, but males were often ordered to fight in local wars. A generous owner might free a thrall who was loyal and hardworking.

WOMEN IN THE VIKING WORLD

Viking women cared for children, cooked, and spun cloth. They also regularly accompanied their husbands abroad, but probably not as warriors. They stayed at camp, cooking meals and tending to the wounded. Still, Viking women had far more power than their sisters abroad. They could own land and ask for a divorce. When the men were away, ill, or dead—all common situations—wives took full charge of running the house and farm.

VIKINGS AT HOME

WHAT DID THE VIKINGS DO WHEN THEY WEREN'T
SAILING SEAS OR SWINGING SWORDS? LIFE AT HOME WAS PERHAPS LESS DANGEROUS,

but it was still hard work. Most Vikings were farmers. They worked long, hard days to try to make a living before winter froze their fields.

A Viking blacksmith made tools and weapons.

EXPLORER'S CORNER

One of the best places to see Viking houses is at Jarlshof, at the southern tip of Scotland's Shetland Islands. People had been living and farming there for about 3,000 years when the Vikings arrived and built their longhouses on top of the ancient remains. Archaeologists have found loom weights for weaving, fishing line weights for deep-sea fishing, and several pictures of Viking ships etched on stone.

HELP WANTED: VIKING WORKERS

FARMER: Grow barley, oats, rye, corn, peas, and cabbage. Raise cattle, goats, pigs, and sheep. Also, hunt seals, whales, elk, and birds; fish for cod, trout, herring, and salmon. Make and repair tools as needed. Join a raid, if time allows.

FARMER'S WIFE: Milk cows. Churn butter and make cheese. Grind grain and bake bread. Roast and stew meat, or pickle and smoke it for winter. Spin wool, sew, and launder clothes. Care for children and the sick.

FARMER'S CHILDREN: Feed animals, gather firewood, and learn all the required skills to take over the farm someday. Both boys and girls will learn to sing, recite poetry, and tell sagas. Learning runes is an added bonus. Boys should learn to use a spear.

CRAFTSMAN: Mold and shape jewelry, blow glass beads and cups, or carve bone and wood.

MERCHANT: Sell jewelry, silk, lace, spices, and slaves at town markets.

SHIPBUILDER: Build warships, trading boats, and fishing craft using the day's most cutting-edge technology.

WEALTHY BOYS: Train with the finest weapons. Practice rowing and sailing. All forms of aggression will be encouraged.

NORSE NOTE VIKINGS SOLD NARWHAL TUSKS TO OTHER EUROPEANS, WHO BELIEVED THE TUSKS CAME FROM UNICORNS.

VIKINGS AT PLAY

When Vikings couldn't work, they played. They passed dark winter nights singing, dancing, reciting poetry, and telling stories about gods and famous battles. They played board games similar to checkers and chess. On snowy days, they skied and skated, using polished bones as blades. In summer, they swam, wrestled, and rode horses. Jesters, jugglers, and musicians amused the rich at feasts all year round.

The cold and snowy Scandinavian winters made cross-country skiing an important way of getting from one place to another. Sagas tell of Norwegian warriors spiriting a king's son to safety while on skis.

A longhouse replica at the L'Anse aux Meadows site in Newfoundland, Canada

LONGHOUSE, SWEET LONGHOUSE

Vikings lived in family groups of three generations or more. Thirty or more people—plus animals—might have lived together in a single longhouse. This classic Viking farmhouse was made of logs, wood planks, or woven branches slathered in mud and animal poop, or dung. Thick grass covered the slanted roof. There were no windows, but smoke holes let some daylight in. The family cooked, ate, and slept by an open fireplace in the main hall. It was probably dark and smelly a lot of the time. Luckily, the outhouse and garbage pit were located away from the house.

Norse Numbers

7 children, on average, were born to each Viking woman.

10 was the age when a wealthy Viking boy received his first real weapons.

12 wasn't too young for a Viking girl to marry.

50 percent of children didn't live to be older than age ten.

55 was a ripe old age to die.

VIKING STYLE

SCROLL THROUGH PHOTOS OF VIKING

ARTIFACTS, AND YOU'RE BOUND TO BE STRUCK BY HOW FANCY their stuff was. Practically every object was an opportunity for decoration, including brooches, cups, tools, weapons, doorways, and so much more. Vikings loved vibrant colors, flashy metalwork, and ornate designs. Such beauty was a sign of status—admired by all, but reserved for the rich.

VIKING ART 101

How can you tell if an object is from the Viking age? Look for some of these trademark features.

GRIPPING BEASTS

Viking sagas mention many beasts such as dragons. They were a huge theme in Viking art. These animals clutch at their own twisted bodies, often with a wicked grin.

FILIGREE

Fine metal wires or beads make intricate raised patterns across a surface.

INTERLACED PATTERNS

Designs look like woven ribbons, knots, or looping rings.

NORSE NOTE VIKING MEN WORE RINGS ON THEIR FINGERS, ARMS, AND SOMETIMES, THEIR NECKS.

PICTURE STONES

These memorial stones were public works of art. Pictures of gods, ships, and warriors, often with accompanying runes, commemorate battles or praise the dearly departed.

Finely decorated Viking brooches were used to attach cloaks or shawls.

DRESS LIKE A KING

We often think of Vikings as chainmail-wearing warriors, but when not warring or raiding, most Vikings dressed in simple wool and linen clothing. Men worked the fields in pants and knee-length tunics, while women went about their daily chores in straight, long dresses. For the upper classes, though, fashion was an opportunity to show off their wealth. Bright colors, luxury fabrics, jewelry, and intricate designs were all hallmarks of Viking high fashion.

Belt buckles, brooches, and armbands added bling for both men and women. They were made of bronze, gold, or silver, and were carved with gripping beasts and complicated designs.

Bright red and blue were especially prized.

Ribbons added color and flair, especially when sewn on with thread made of real gold.

A rich man's cloak might be lined with marmot fur.

Silk was a sure sign of high class. The precious fabric was imported from the East.

Embroidered designs were another way to add color and interest.

RIDE WITH THE VALKYRIES

IF YOU CAN STOMACH IT,

PICTURE A VIKING BATTLE. HUNDREDS of men stab, slash, and hack at each other—the clash of weapons is deafening. Arrows rain down from the sky. Blood soaks the ground. But above all these horrors, a Viking warrior feared something far more frightening: showing cowardice. As long as he could control his nerves, victory was his. If he died honorably, he believed a glorious afterlife awaited him. If he survived, then fame and riches were his.

THE NORSE ADVANTAGE

They attacked like "stinging hornets." Viking raiders arrived in swarms. They hit hard. Then they left just as suddenly. In their quest for riches, Vikings burned, killed, and kidnapped—not even women and children were spared. Often, just the threat of a raid was enough to get villagers to empty their pockets. But really, Viking raiders were no more ruthless than other European warriors. Their weapons and tactics were pretty standard, too. Their advantage came down to their amazing warships. Those longships allowed them to glide up rivers and dash in and out of harbors. Viking raiders were masters of surprise.

Longships often had fearsome dragon-head prows.

120 VIKING SHIPS CARRIED **THOUSANDS** OF **WARRIORS** DOWN THE **RIVER SEINE** DURING THE **VIKING RAID** OF **PARIS** IN A.D. **845.**

NORSE NOTE SOME VIKING WARRIORS FILED GROOVES IN THE FRONT OF THEIR TEETH TO LOOK TOUGH.

Valkyries were said to have long flowing hair.

DEATH DEALERS

Valkyries were mythical women who worked for Odin, the Norse god of war. These beautiful maidens selected which warriors would receive the honor of dying in battle. The Valkyries then carried the chosen men's souls to Valhalla—Odin's glorious hall. There, the beautiful Valkyries pampered the lucky men with the finest food and drink.

FOUR WAYS TO RAID

Raiding parties used these common maneuvers:

EASY PREY

Snatched a fishing boat or grabbed cattle grazing by the shore. No violence was required.

HALL BURNING

Stationed men by the entrances of a wealthy family's house and set fire to the roof. Killed family members as they fled, then snatched loot.

MONASTERIES

Covered entrances, then attacked. Captured monks as they tried to run away. The monks made fine slaves and fetched high ransoms.

TOWNS

Attacked swiftly before townspeople hid their treasure. If necessary, torture persuaded locals to turn over their riches.

BURIED IN A BOAT?

Most Vikings were buried in simple coffins or shrouds, but the wealthy and powerful were often entombed in boats. Mourners first filled the boats with the dead person's weapons, tools, and other everyday possessions—sometimes including servants and dogs. The well-stocked boat was meant to carry provisions for the afterlife. Today, these boat burials, when found, are rich sources of historic Viking artifacts.

Finely carved wooden furniture has been found in burial boats.

Threatened by Vikings, some foreign rulers paid them to "make peace" instead of war.

A PHOTO GALLERY

VIKING REENACTMENTS

WANT TO TAKE PART IN A VIKING FEAST?

Or relive a Viking battle (minus the blood and guts)? Viking museums and history fans re-create Viking life through festivals and reenactments in which amateur actors dress up like real-life Norsemen to learn what Viking life was like a thousand years ago.

A lot of research goes into making a historically correct Viking costume with battle helmets, swords, and chainmail.

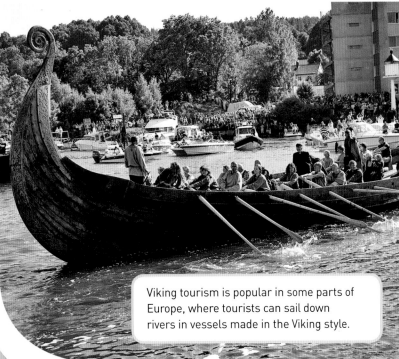

Viking tourism is popular in some parts of Europe, where tourists can sail down rivers in vessels made in the Viking style.

These volunteers are taking part in a reenactment of the Battle of York in England, where the Vikings fought the English.

The Guizer Jarl leads a parade of marching Vikings during the Up Helly Aa festival in Lerwick, on the Shetland Islands in Scotland. Vikings settled on the island, and every year the festival is celebrated with a giant bonfire.

A woman demonstrates Viking shoemaking at a Viking museum in York, England.

Museum interpreters dress and act as Vikings at the Viking settlement site at L'Anse aux Meadows, Newfoundland.

Viking raids were sudden, swift, and brutal. Villages and monasteries that were raided were not warned and had no time to prepare or defend. This made the raids a profitable way for Vikings to increase their wealth by stealing goods and enslaving people.

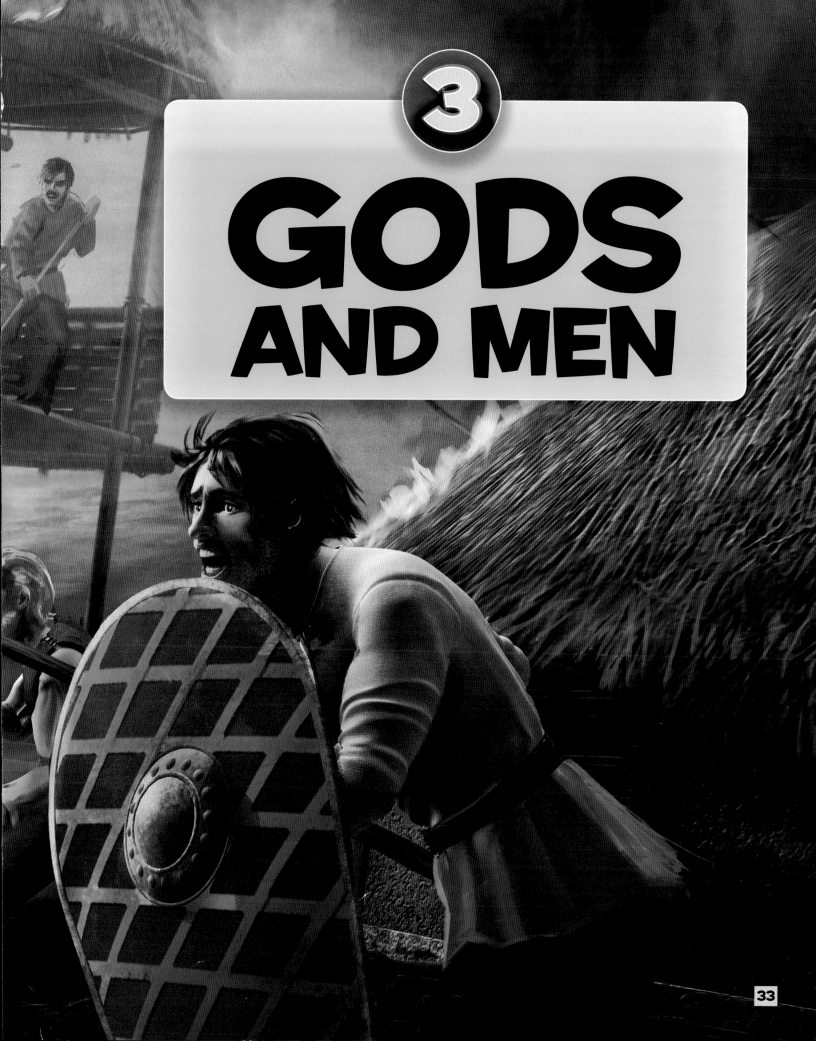

3

GODS
AND MEN

THE VIKING GODS

AS A VIKING, YOU DIDN'T "BELIEVE IN" GODS. GODS WERE JUST A PART OF NATURE, LIKE A MOUNTAIN OR A LAKE, AND THEY COULD BE AS

foolish as humans. Vikings performed rituals to please the mighty spirits. In turn, the gods rewarded them with good crops or smooth sailing. Religious ceremonies took place at home, outside, or in a nobleman's hall. Pleasing the gods was a good daily habit for everyone, kind of like brushing your teeth.

WORLDS UPON WORLDS

Vikings saw the universe as many overlapping worlds. Mortals occupied Midgard, located in the middle of the cosmos. The gods lived in Asgard, which, in turn, housed a dozen or more personal homes of the gods. The dead could end up in any number of realms, while evil giants lurked in the wilderness. At the end of time, giants would defeat the gods in the battle of Ragnarok, and new worlds would begin.

Odin means "furious one" in the Old Norse language.

The Norns are weaving the rope of destiny.

NORNS

In some ways, the Norns were the most powerful beings of all. These three sisters decided the date of every being's death, including the gods. Belief in the Norns may have made it easier for a Viking to face battle. After all, his destiny had been written the day he was born.

MEET THE GODS

ODIN, father of the gods; also god of war, poetry, and wisdom. Clever and dangerous, Odin can change shape, raise the dead, and see into the future. His two pet ravens, Thought and Memory, report to him daily with news of the human realm.

THOR, god of physical strength, weather, and crops. This beloved god makes thunder by throwing his magic hammer. Viking men wore a charm of Thor's hammer around their neck for good luck.

FREY, god of farming and fertility. Farmers painted Frey's image on their wagons to make their crops thrive.

BALDER, god of goodness, beauty, and light. Only one thing can harm him—mistletoe. In one Viking legend, Loki finds a way to kill Balder with his one weakness.

FREYA, goddess of love and beauty but also of war and death. She rules over Folkvangr, where half the warriors who die in battle go to rest.

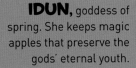

IDUN, goddess of spring. She keeps magic apples that preserve the gods' eternal youth.

LOKI, trickster god. Loki changes form, usually to cause trouble for other gods.

NORSE NOTE VIKINGS OPENED BATTLE BY THROWING A SPEAR OVER THE ENEMY. THIS HONORED ODIN AND HIS MAGICAL SPEAR, GUNGNIR.

FAMOUS VIKINGS

THEY MAY NOT HAVE BEEN GODS,
BUT THEIR NAMES AND LEGENDS LIVE ON. THESE

Viking explorers, warriors, and kings are still remembered today—for better or worse.

LEIF ERIKSSON

Leif, son of Erik the Red, set sail from Greenland to the shores of North America around 1000. He discovered a land he called Vinland, which means Land of the Wine, presumably because of the wild grapes he found here. Historians still argue about Vinland's exact location and whether those grapes were really berries.

ERIK THE RED

After killing two of his neighbor's sons in Iceland, this famously red-headed Viking needed to get out of town quickly. In A.D. 986, he led a party of settlers westward to a huge, icy island. Erik named the forbidding land "Greenland" in the hope of enticing newcomers.

ERIK BLOODAXE

Erik Bloodaxe proves that even Vikings had their limit when it came to violence. Erik was kicked off the throne of Norway in the A.D. 930s for killing too many rivals—including seven of his brothers.

> "CATTLE DIE AND KINSMEN DIE, AND SO DOES ONE'S SELF, ONE THING I KNOW THAT NEVER DIES, THE FAME OF A MAN'S DEEDS."
> —FROM THE VIKING POEM, THE HÁVAMÁL

NORSE NOTE A VIKING MAN WAS BURIED WITH A BROKEN SWORD SO HIS GHOST COULDN'T USE IT AGAINST THE LIVING.

FREYDIS ERIKSDOTTIR

Freydis traveled to Vinland shortly after her brother, Leif Eriksson. According to one saga, Freydis was a murderess who cheated the ship she was on out of its cargo. In another saga, she saved the day by single-handedly thwarting an attack.

CNUT THE GREAT

This Danish-born king's empire included England, Denmark, Norway, and part of Sweden. He was the son of Sweyn Forkbeard, king of Denmark. Cnut, also known as Canute, inherited his father's kingdom after his brother died. Cnut worked hard to build his kingdom. He conquered England with a fleet of 200 longships in 1015. The empire collapsed when Cnut died in 1035.

BJÖRN IRONSIDE AND HASTEIN

These Viking brothers led a fleet of 60 ships along the coasts of France, Spain, North Africa, and Italy. From A.D. 859 to A.D. 862, they seized a huge fortune, only to lose most of their ships in storms on the way home.

OLEG OF KIEV

This Swedish ruler already controlled large areas of Russian land when he set out for Constantinople, in what is now Turkey, in A.D. 907. His huge army scared the Byzantines so much, they paid him just to keep the peace. Oleg took the deal and also opened up trading rights in Constantinople.

JELLING STONE

HARALD BLUETOOTH

In the A.D. 960s, King Harald united Danish tribes into one kingdom. Other claims to fame include the first bridge in Scandinavia, as well as the most famous Viking monument—the Jelling stones.

HOW TO BE A VIKING WARRIOR

SO, YOU'RE A GLORY SEEKER,

ARE YOU? AND, LUCKY YOU, YOU'RE WEALTHY

enough to leave your Viking farm for a while. You're off with the next fleet on a raid across the sea. It's not a job for the faint of heart, mind you. In their quest for riches, your fellow raiders will kill, torture, and kidnap—women and children will not be spared. Nor will you be, perhaps. You have about a 50-50 chance of making it back home. May the god Thor protect you!

GET BACK OUT THERE AND FIND SOME TREASURE!

Women were standard members of a raiding party. They stayed at camp to do the washing and cooking—just like at home. But they had another special role. No man wanted to appear a coward before his wife or favorite slave girl. The women shamed the men into fighting harder.

Treasure included silver jewelry.

BURYING LOOTED TREASURE

Getting killed in a raid was a real threat—but just one of many. Raiders also faced shipwreck, deadly diarrhea, and starvation. Sore feet, fatigue, and boredom were also part of the deal. Even if you were lucky enough to end up with a bag of riches, theft became a constant worry. Some raiders chose to bury their loot in holes, like squirrels hiding acorns. Many were never able to return to collect their treasures. These treasure troves, known as Viking hoards, are still being discovered today.

DON'T FORGET THE AX

Before setting sail, a smart Viking might take these measures to ensure a successful raid:

- ✓ Wear Thor's hammer charm around neck to avoid shipwreck.
- ✓ Check with a soothsayer to see if gods are for or against the trip.
- ✓ Talk to exiles and traveling merchants for news about famines, wars, and other events that could affect travel plans.

NORSE NOTE RAIDERS GREASED THEIR IRON WEAPONS AND TIED THEM IN SEALSKIN BAGS TO PREVENT SEAWATER FROM RUSTING THE

GEAR UP

Vikings didn't have uniforms. They battled with what they could afford. Many got by with just a spear, shield, leather shirt, and helmet. A rich warrior had a sword, shield, chainmail shirt, and iron helmet.

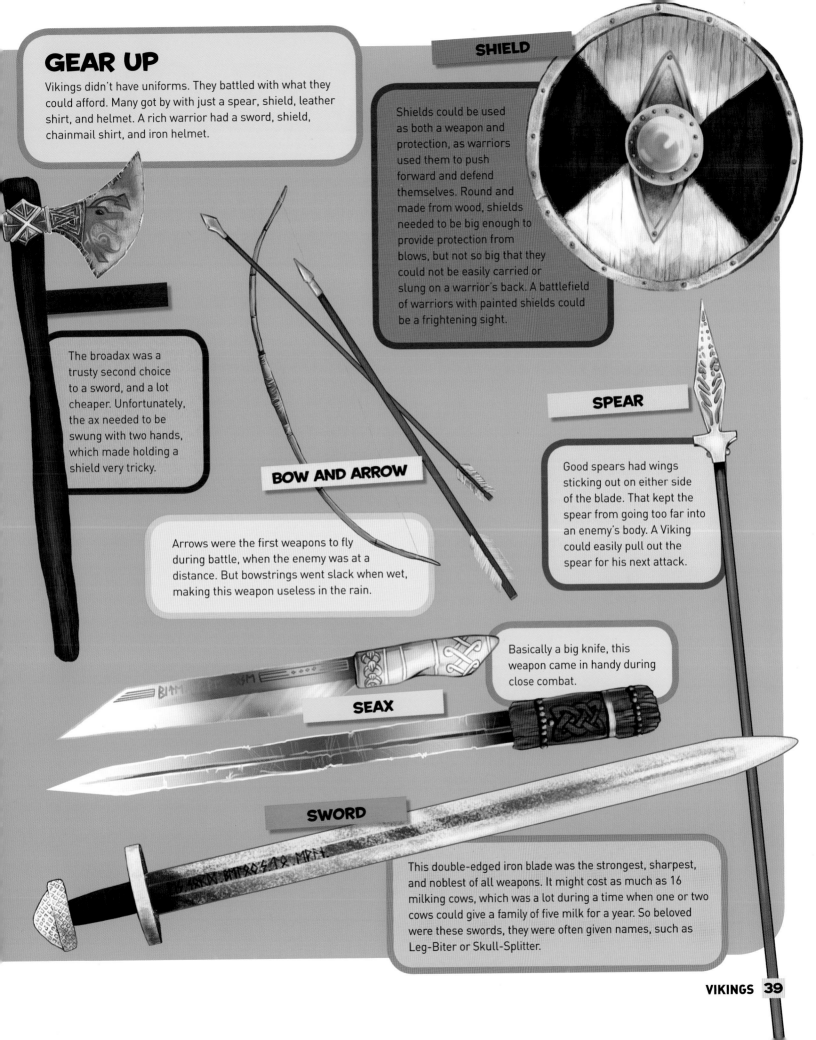

SHIELD

Shields could be used as both a weapon and protection, as warriors used them to push forward and defend themselves. Round and made from wood, shields needed to be big enough to provide protection from blows, but not so big that they could not be easily carried or slung on a warrior's back. A battlefield of warriors with painted shields could be a frightening sight.

BROADAX

The broadax was a trusty second choice to a sword, and a lot cheaper. Unfortunately, the ax needed to be swung with two hands, which made holding a shield very tricky.

SPEAR

Good spears had wings sticking out on either side of the blade. That kept the spear from going too far into an enemy's body. A Viking could easily pull out the spear for his next attack.

BOW AND ARROW

Arrows were the first weapons to fly during battle, when the enemy was at a distance. But bowstrings went slack when wet, making this weapon useless in the rain.

Basically a big knife, this weapon came in handy during close combat.

SEAX

SWORD

This double-edged iron blade was the strongest, sharpest, and noblest of all weapons. It might cost as much as 16 milking cows, which was a lot during a time when one or two cows could give a family of five milk for a year. So beloved were these swords, they were often given names, such as Leg-Biter or Skull-Splitter.

VIKINGS LIVE ON

VIKING POETS LIT UP DARK WINTER NIGHTS RECITING

EPICS OF BLOODY BATTLES AND FEARSOME WARRIORS. BUT BY 1100, THOSE STORIES probably seemed more like folktales than newspaper headlines. The age of Vikings had faded away. What happened to the Vikings?

NEW WORLD ORDER

By the end of the Viking age, the Vikings had run out of easy targets, and they had only themselves to blame. Their usual targets in Britain and other areas rallied together against the Viking warriors. Back at home, Denmark, Norway, and Sweden had also become wealthy and stable kingdoms. A Viking man had new opportunities at home. He didn't need to go abroad to seek his fortune or escape local feuds.

After the Viking age, the descendants of the Vikings farmed the fertile lands of Scandinavia, just as many of their ancestors did. They raised animals and harvested wheat, oats, barley, and rye, as well as root vegetables.

NORSE NOTE STORNOWAY, IN SCOTLAND'S OUTER HEBRIDES, IS OLD NORSE FOR "STEERING BAY."

Over time, Vikings who settled in places such as Ireland, Scotland, and western and eastern Europe blended in with the local people. Some Vikings settled islands such as the Faroes, in the North Atlantic Ocean. This statue in Gota, Faroe Islands, commemorates a Viking from the Islands whose history is written in a Viking saga.

WHAT HAPPENED TO GREENLAND?

Two Viking colonies survived in Greenland for 500 years before they vanished in the 15th century. Nobody knows exactly why, but it probably had something to do with a mini ice age that began around 1350. Vikings could no longer make a living with an even harsher winter and trade routes blocked by ice. They may have been pushed out by the Thule peoples, ancestors of the Inuit, coming down from the north.

The Bayeux Tapestry is an embroidered cloth that shows the Norman Conquest of England by William I, or William the Conqueror, a descendant of the Vikings who became king of England.

EXPLORER'S CORNER

Shetlanders are proud to be descended from the Vikings, and every winter they celebrate their heritage, lighting up the dark January nights with fire at the Up Helly Aa festival. About a thousand men in many squads, carrying flaming torches, parade through the streets of Lerwick. They set fire to a longship which has been lovingly built and painted over the previous year. The members of the main squad, led by the Guizer Jarl, dress as Vikings. After the ship has been consumed by the fire, they head off to the halls, where they dance until the morning.

THE NORMANS

One group of Vikings, known as the Normans, made France their special target. By A.D. 911, French King Charles the Simple was so fed up with all the raiding and pillaging that he gave a chunk of northern France, known as Normandy, to the Viking leader Rollo. All Charles asked in return was some peace and quiet. Charles's plan worked—for a while, at least. The Normans adopted the Christian religion and the French language, but they never lost their Norse thirst for conquest. By the mid-tenth century, the Normans were at it again. Normandy's famed duke, William the Conqueror, captured England in the Battle of Hastings in 1066. The Norman Conquest of England paved the way for the England we know today.

VIKING COMPARISONS

NEXT TIME YOU
NEED TO GET DRESSED UP

like a Viking, don't get caught in something from the wrong century. Use this handy guide to compare today's trends with Viking fashions.

YOU VS. A VIKING

WINTER COAT

In winter, Vikings wore heavy wool or shaggy fur cloaks. The cloaks were fastened by ties or with a brooch. A warrior pinned his over the right shoulder to keep his sword arm free.

PANTS

Men wore the pants in Viking society. Woolen pants, not unlike today's, were common. Other pants were long and fitted like skinny jeans, or they billowed out at the knees. Men topped their pants with knee-length tunics, belted around the waist. A rich man's tunic might be trimmed with silk, or a colorful woven braid.

HELMETS

It's important to protect your head, whether you're riding a bike or dodging swords. Vikings didn't ride bikes, but they still tried to protect their heads—at least when swords were coming at them. Most men got by with a simple leather helmet. Wealthy men traded up for metal.

BROOCHES

Forget buttons, zippers, hooks, or elastic. Viking women held up their wool dresses with matching oval shoulder brooches. A third brooch might hold a cloak below her neck. She'd festoon, or hang, silver, crystal, or amber beads between her brooches, if she could afford them. Today, brooches are mostly just for decoration.

SHOES AND SOCKS

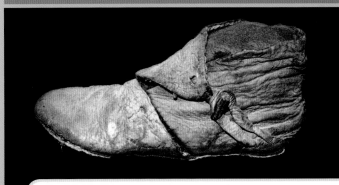

Your favorite pair of kicks might be made of leather or canvas, and are probably designed to suit a specific sport or activity. Chances are that the socks you wear with them are made from comfy, cozy cotton. For Vikings, "shoe technology" meant calfskin or goatskin booties that tied around the ankle. Men's and women's styles looked pretty much the same. A rich person might enjoy a fine pair of wool socks inside his or her shoes. The rest made do with stuffing dry grass or moss under their toes.

A typical Viking feast might include roast meat, salted fish, bread, and fruit, all eaten on wooden plates, with knives and spoons as utensils. Vikings also drank beer, or mead made with honey, sometimes from animal horns.

44

4
VIKING GAMES

WHICH VIKING GOD ARE YOU?

NORSE, OR VIKING, GODS HAD FLAWS JUST LIKE MORTAL HUMANS. THEY WERE PLAYFUL, SELFISH, VENGEFUL, FOOLISH, AND

occasionally silly. Are you a trickster, or a leader? Take this handy quiz to see which deity is your double.

1 **What do you like to do in your spare time?**

A. read
B. make art
C. lift weights
D. prank your friends

2 **What do you like to read most?**

A. the classics
B. love stories
C. the weather report
D. comic books

3 **What do you fear most?**

A. wolves
B. losing someone you love
C. snakes
D. earthquakes

4 **What would you like to be when you grow up?**

A. president
B. party planner
C. bodybuilder
D. reality TV show producer

5 **What cause is most important to you?**

A. a strong military
B. promoting the arts
C. feeding the hungry
D. Who cares?

6 **What magic power would you choose?**

A. total knowledge of past, present, and future
B. making people fall in love
C. amazing physical strength
D. shape-shifting

7 **What's your worst quality?**

A. being too competitive
B. spending too much money
C. not thinking things through
D. Who wants to know?

8 **What's your favorite animal?**

A. horse
B. cat
C. goat
D. the one on my plate

IF YOU SCORED MOSTLY

A's: You are Odin. Odin is the boss of gods. He rules war and poetry. He literally gave up an eye for wisdom. Odin made the world—and he thinks the world of himself, too. Don't expect Odin to get off his eight-legged horse to help you in a time of need. But if he does, you'll have it made. Despite his awesome power, Viking legend says that Odin gets eaten by a wolf at the end of the world.

ODIN

ERIK THE RED

D. MYTH Actually, Vikings were, on average, three to four inches (8 to 10 cm) shorter than we are today. (Given their lifestyles, they were probably more muscular and had more scars, though.) Blonds dominated in Scandinavia, but plenty of brown-haired (or brunet) and a few red-haired Vikings went about their business, too.

E. FACT Leif Eriksson, also known as Leif the Lucky, sailed from Greenland to the northeast coast of North America around 1000. That's 500 years before Christopher Columbus.

VIKINGS
PAST AND PRESENT

THE VIKINGS STOPPED RAIDING MORE THAN 900 YEARS
AGO, BUT THEY STILL HOLD US SPELLBOUND. BEGINNING IN THE 19TH CENTURY,

Vikings took off in popular culture. Since then, they've popped up in everything from comic books to space probes.

1870s

German composer Richard Wagner catapults Vikings into popular imagination with the Ring Cycle—four operas based on Norse mythology. Costume designers dressed actors in horned helmets.

1955

J. R. R. Tolkien publishes the final volume of *The Lord of the Rings*. The fantasy takes place in Middle-earth, a land based on the Viking idea of Midgard—the world of mortals.

1961

The Minnesota Vikings football team play their first game ever. Like real Vikings, they wear helmets, but theirs are purple with painted horns on the sides.

1962

Thor, the beloved Norse god of lightning and thunder, becomes a superhero in Marvel comic books. Thor still defeats evil with his magic hammer, but he wears a new red cape.

1973

The comic strip "Hägar the Horrible" appears on newspaper comic pages. Hägar, Helga, and Lucky Eddie become history's most lovable cartoon Vikings.

VIKING 1

"HÄGAR THE HORRIBLE"

1976

Named in honor of the great Scandinavian explorers, Viking 1 is the first spacecraft ever to touch down on Mars.

FREYA

IF YOU SCORED MOS

C's: You are Thor. Ah, Thor, s
(though maybe just a little du
to lend a hand with crops or crea
for a god, he's larger than life. He
lightning with his magic hammer
sky in a goat-drawn chariot. One
the other gods from evil giants. Ev
a snake at the end of the world.

IF YOU SCORED MOSTLY

B's: You are Freya. Count on Freya for help with love, beauty, and magic. She also has a powerful hand in fertility and childbirth. Freya likes fine things, and she wears a golden necklace that was forged by magical creatures. Other favorite possessions include her cat-drawn chariot and a feather cloak that turns the wearer into a bird. Freya roams the world seeking her lost husband, while weeping tears of gold.

LOKI

IF YOU SCORED MOSTLY

D's: You are Loki. The trickster god, Loki is an amazing shape-shifter. Loki can make everybody laugh, but he definitely goes too far. After one trick too many, the gods tied him up in a cave for all time, where a snake drips venom over him. His wife catches most of the drips, but she has to leave to empty her bowl. As the poison drips on Loki, he begins to writhe and shake, which causes earthquakes.

NORSE NOTE IN THE VIKING AFTERLIFE, WOM

THE REAL VIKING

ASE STAND UP?

MYTH VS. FACT

A. MYTH

Are you trying to start a fight? Insulting a Viking's hygiene could be cause for a brawl! Vikings washed every morning and bathed every Saturday. They also combed their hair (and/or beards) daily to remove lice and nits. Tweezers, nail cleaners, ear cleaners, and toothpicks have all been found at Viking sites. Still, without dentistry, most Vikings probably had many rotten teeth.

want to
f horned
rd Wagner in
ps, or domed
o of metal hung

G PRIDE. CALLING ANOTHER MAN "BEARDLESS" WAS A MAJOR INSULT.

2010

The animated movie *How to Train Your Dragon* introduces a Viking boy named Hiccup. He becomes a hero by making friends with a misunderstood enemy.

2012

In *The Avengers*, Thor and his superhero allies save the world from Loki and his evil cohorts. This Norse-based blockbuster becomes one of the top-grossing Hollywood movies of all time.

2014

In a controversial twist, a Marvel comic book series turns Thor into a woman.

THOR

WHAT'S YOUR VIKING NICKNAME?

Congratulations! Just being given a name in Viking culture meant that you were strong. Sickly babies were left to die without naming ceremonies.

Chances are you'd be named after a relative or ancestor. Your last name came from your father's first name. Boys added -*son*, as in Leif Eriksson (son of Erik the Red). Girls added -*dottir*, as in Freydis Eriksdottir (daughter of Erik the Red).

Vikings also loved nicknames. These might describe how they looked (Helgi the Lean) or acted (Thord the Bellower). Or they could simply be a telling turn of phrase (Erik Bloodaxe).

The words below are all from real Viking names. Follow the steps to create your own Viking nickname.

1. START WITH YOUR OWN FIRST NAME.

2. ADD "THE."

3. ADD AN ADJECTIVE.

Bare	Fair	Lucky	Slippery
Black	Fine	Old	Snobbish
Bold	Frosty	Raving	Swift
Broad	Hateful	Red	Tough
Careful	Lean	Shy	White
Clever	Little	Skinny	Yellow

4. ADD A NOUN.

Ax	Fool	Legs	Serpent
Bard	Foot	Poet	Star
Beard	Goat	Riddler	Tongue
Blood	Head	Roarer	Troll
Clanger	Horse	Screamer	Yeller

5. MAKE IT YOURS

Maybe you came up with *Morgan the Swiftax*. Delete the "the" to make *Morgan Swiftax*. Doesn't that sound better? Or how about just *Morgan the Swift*? Two nouns make a nice combo, too. Who wouldn't want to meet *Ella Goatlegs*, or *Cecilia the Headscreamer*?

WHAT DID YOU SAY?

TO BE AN ACCOMPLISHED VIKING, YOU HAD TO BE
STRONG, BRAVE, SKILLED, AND CLEVER. BUT A TRUE VIKING VIRTUOSO ALSO SHOWED
a flair for words. After all, poets and storytellers were the main event at feasts and celebrations. You also had to have a pretty good memory. Until the 12th century, stories and poems were told, not written. If you were lucky, you knew how to carve runes, or Norse writing. These sacred symbols were a gift from the god Odin. Rune masters knew how to harness their secret power to create magic and read the future. The 16 characters also served as an alphabet. Vikings carved short rune messages on sticks, metal, and stone.

Rune stones marked territory or honored dead relatives.

A HARD CODE TO CRACK

Even experts have trouble decoding runes. Note that a single rune could mean several different letters. Not only that, but what is shown here is just one version of the runes. There were several others. Runes can read left to right, or right to left, or upside down. And forget about punctuation!

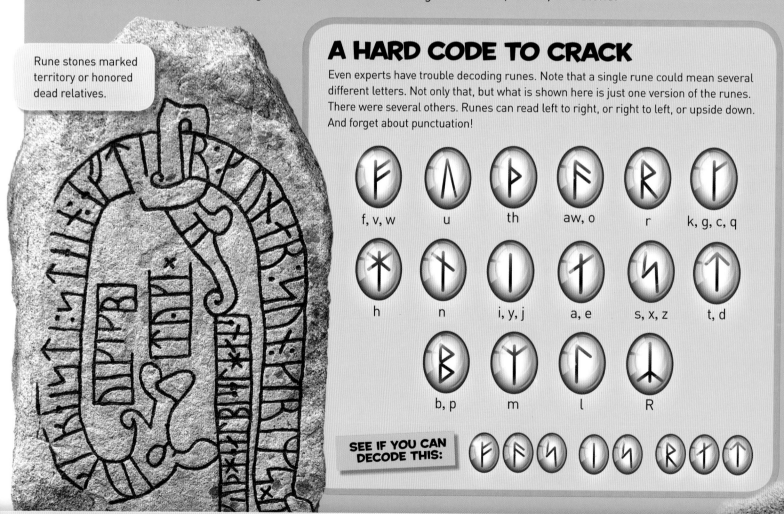

f, v, w | u | th | aw, o | r | k, g, c, q

h | n | i, y, j | a, e | s, x, z | t, d

b, p | m | l | R

SEE IF YOU CAN DECODE THIS:

NORSE NOTE SOME VIKING CON MEN WENT AROUND TOSSING INSULTS ON PURPOSE AND MADE A LIVING BY WINNING DUELS.

ANSWER: Fox is red

FIGHTING WORDS

Oh, horror! Someone insulted you at a feast last night. They called you a "beardless oath-breaker" ... Or was it "fearless bath-faker"? In any case, you won't stand for it! Walking away from an insult is almost as dishonorable as fleeing a fight. Answer these questions to figure out what to do.

NO ← **ARE YOU A STRONG FIGHTER?** → **YES**

YES ← **Are you wealthy?** → **NO**

YES ← **Are you good with words?** → **NO**

Are you planning to move to Iceland or Greenland soon? **YES** →

NO ↓

Challenge your enemy to a flyting, or public exchange of insults. The audience chooses the winner. You'd better be witty, or you'll end up looking like a fool.

Are you SURE? Lots of outlaws and social misfits find a fresh start abroad.

You don't want to resort to violence. If you harm your opponent, you'll have to pay a hefty fine. It will also probably start a blood feud with your victim's family. Good thing you're moving.

You could call for a duel, or *hólmganga*. Settling a disagreement with combat was one Viking solution. Agree carefully on the rules beforehand, especially for what counts as losing. If you win, the loser has to pay you in silver.

TEST YOUR SKALDIC SKILLS

A skald, or professional poet, shouted out poems in the midst of battle. He made up the poems on the spot. It gets tiring using the same old words all the time, though. So skalds used kennings, or metaphors, to keep their poems fresh. Can you match the following kennings to their meaning?

1. SHIELD DANGER
2. WEAPON STORM
3. SKY'S BLOOD
4. BATTLE SWEAT
5. SWORD'S SLEEP
6. WHALE'S ROAD
7. FEEDER OF THE WOLF
8. WAR NEEDLES

A. WARRIOR
B. ARROWS
C. BLOOD
D. AX
E. THE SEA
F. DEATH
G. RAIN
H. BATTLE

ANSWERS: 1. d; 2. h; 3. g; 4. c; 5. f; 6. e; 7. a; 8. b

THANK THOR IT'S THURSDAY!

Thursday was a feast day in Viking culture. It was a day to honor their favorite god, Thor. *Thor's day* became Thursday in English. We also honor Odin, aka Woden, on *Woden's day* (Wednesday) and Odin's wife Frigg on *Frigg's day*, or Friday.

PHOTO FINISH

NOTHING PREPARES YOU

FOR THE SPLENDOR OF THE OSEBERG SHIP, THE most amazing treasure to have survived from the Viking age—an actual Viking ship!

I have been lucky enough to visit it several times, and each time it takes my breath away. It is housed in the Viking Ship Museum in Norway's capital city, Oslo. It was discovered in 1903 by a farmer named Knut Rom when he dug into a burial mound on his farm. He was astonished to find a ship. After the archaeological excavation, it took 21 years to preserve the ship, and today 90 percent of its timbers are still original.

We now know a lot about the ship. It was constructed of oak and built in western Norway about A.D. 820. The mast is made of pine and was between 32 and 43 feet (10 and 13 m) high. It was pulled ashore in A.D. 834 and used for a spectacular burial. What's really interesting is that the two people who were buried in it were not Viking warriors, but important Viking women. One was about 70 to 80 years old, and the other was probably a little over 50. Perhaps one was a queen and the other a priestess. They were laid out on a bed in the burial chamber. Around them were hung extraordinary tapestries and many objects for the next life.

It was clearly believed that these noble Viking women were going somewhere after death and that they needed to have their belongings, such as their combs, shoes, and clothing, with them. The Oseberg burial ship also contained the ship's equipment, kitchen and farm equipment, a wagon, five carved animal heads, five beds and two tents, and, for the snow—four sleighs.

When you stand beside the Oseberg ship, it's a bit like traveling in time—you are as close as it's possible to be to the Vikings.

Grave goods in the burial ship include finely carved and decorated sleighs, a cart, and beautiful ship posts.

The excavated Oseberg ship can be seen at the Viking Ship Museum in Norway.

AFTERWORD

LIKE ANY GREAT ACTION MOVIE, THE STORY OF THE VIKING AGE HAS A TWIST. THE

tale begins with bands of men who sail abroad to raid and conquer. But by the end, the ruthless destroyers have left a legacy surprisingly full of promise.

The Vikings globalized their world. Across Europe and beyond, they opened people's eyes to new methods and ideas. Thank the Vikings for introducing the world's oldest parliament in Iceland. Courtroom juries, which began in England, can also be traced to Viking ideas of justice.

The Vikings helped organize Europe into kingdoms. They founded Iceland, for one. They also forced fiefdoms to unite, raise armies, and collect taxes to meet the Viking threat. Thank the Vikings for a map of Europe that still looks familiar today.

Thank Viking traders for cities such as Dublin, Ireland; York, England; and Kiev, Ukraine. Give them credit for introducing a money system to Europe. The Vikings brought in enough silver to mint coins, making bartering a thing of the past.

The Vikings changed the very core of the English language. Words such as happy, husband, bread, and eggs have Norse roots. Think of those bearded warriors the next time you look outside or up in the sky. Now that you know EVERYTHING about Vikings, do you find them odd, sly, wrong, flawed, or awesome? You can thank the Vikings for those words as well.

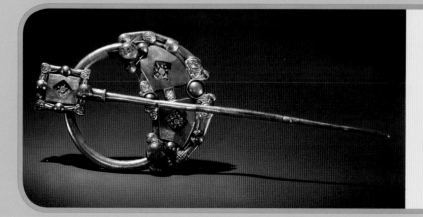

DIGGING THE VIKINGS

Imagine taking your metal detector out to a churchyard and finding a Viking hoard buried 1,000 years ago. It's not as far-fetched as it sounds. In fact, amateur archaeologists have found such treasures. The Vale of York Hoard, a Viking treasure of 617 coins and jewelry, was discovered in 2007 near Harrogate, England. In 2014, buried Viking loot was found in a Scottish churchyard by a treasure hunter with a metal detector. The found treasure is often given to museums.

Russian painter Wassily Kandinsky's 1906 painting "Volga Song" depicts Vikings on the Volga River in Russia.

Viking festivals are still celebrated wherever Vikings settled throughout the world.

AN INTERACTIVE GLOSSARY

VIKING VOCABULARY

Vikings were excellent carvers, transforming oak and other woods into creatures from their mythology, such as dragons and trolls.

LET'S RAID SOME VIKING VOCABULARY!
ARE YOU READY TO SEIZE SOME NEW WORDS BY THE HORNS? USE THE
glossary to learn each new definition, and visit the page numbers to see how the word was used. Then, test your Viking knowledge.

1. Berserker
A Viking warrior who fought in a frenzied trance in the name of Odin (PAGE 15)

A berserker prepared for battle by:

a. shrieking

b. leaping around

c. taking a mind-altering substance

d. all of the above

2. Brooch
A decorative pin
(PAGES 26, 27, 42, 43)

Why were brooches so important to Vikings?

a. they were used in religious rituals

b. they were secret weapons

c. they were fasteners, much like zippers and buttons are today

d. they were hair ornaments

3. Hoard
A stash of buried Viking treasure
(PAGES 11, 38, 56)

Which items are you NOT likely to find in a Viking hoard?

a. silver coins

b. gold armbands

c. filigree brooches

d. acorns

4. Jarl
A Viking nobleman (pronounced "yarl")
(PAGES 22, 23)

Besides jarls, what were the other two main social classes in Viking society?

a. karls and thralls

b. berserkers and Valkyries

c. warriors and skalds

d. kings and fools

5. Longship
A Viking warrior ship (PAGES 13, 18-19, 28)

What made longships exceptional warships?

a. plenty of cargo space for hauling weapons

b. they were easy to maneuver during surprise attacks

c. wide hulls shielded Vikings from arrows

d. they looked like fishing boats to fool enemies

6. Longhouse
A Viking farmhouse was composed mostly of one big room, no windows, and a grass roof (PAGE 25)

How many Viking family members might live together in a single longhouse?

a. 10 to 12

b. 15 to 20

c. up to 30

d. 30 or more

7. Monastery
A place where monks live and work (PAGES 11, 12, 17, 29, 32)

Which monastery attack kicked off the Viking age?

a. Tintern Abbey

b. Mont Saint Michel Abbey

c. Monastery of Lindisfarne

d. St. Anthony Monastery

8. Old Norse
The language spoken by Vikings (PAGES 10, 11, 13, 17, 34, 40)

What modern language is remarkably similar to Old Norse?

a. Swedish

b. Icelandic

c. Danish

d. Norwegian

9. Rune
A letter in the Viking alphabet; a sacred symbol from the god Odin (PAGES 11, 24, 27, 52)

How many runes existed during the Viking age?

a. 26

b. 16

c. 42

d. 10

10. Saga
A story, written in Old Norse, about Viking adventures and gods
(PAGES 11, 17, 24, 25, 26, 37, 41)

When were the sagas written down?

a. around A.D. 800, when the Viking age began

b. around 1000, when the Vikings arrived in North America

c. starting in the 12th century, shortly after the Viking age

d. starting in the 17th century, as the medieval era wound down

11. Skald
A Viking poet who entertained at feasts and inspired warriors in the midst of battle (PAGE 53)

Poetry was one of many Viking pastimes, which included all of the following EXCEPT:

a. board games

b. skiing

c. magic tricks

d. horseback riding

ANSWERS: 1. d; 2. c; 3. d; 4. a; 5. b; 6. c; 7. c; 8. b; 9. b; 10. c; 11. c

FIND OUT MORE

Voyage back to the Viking age with these websites, movies, and more.

VIKING WEBSITES

Kids: Ask your parents for permission to search online.

BBC History
A straightforward overview of Viking topics, written by experts. Perfect for reports.
bbc.co.uk/history/ancient/vikings/

Jorvik Viking Centre
Activities and fun facts from one of the world's most famous Viking museums.
jorvik-viking-centre.co.uk/who-were-the-vikings/activities-and-facts/

National Museum of Denmark
The National Museum of Denmark offers an interactive timeline, videos, and plenty of facts about the Viking age.
en.natmus.dk/museums/the-national-museum-of-denmark/exhibitions/the-danish-prehistory

Smithsonian National Museum of Natural History
Take a virtual tour of the Smithsonian exhibit, "Vikings: The North Atlantic Saga."
mnh.si.edu/vikings/start.html

BLOCKBUSTER MOVIES

*The Avengers**
Marvel Studios, 2012

How to Train Your Dragon
DreamWorks, 2010

How to Train Your Dragon 2
DreamWorks, 2014

*Thor**
Paramount Pictures, 2011

*Thor: The Dark World**
Marvel Studios, 2013

*** Rated PG-13**

DOCUMENTARIES

The Vikings
PBS, 2006

The Vikings: Dark Warriors
A&E Home Video, 2014

READ IT!

The Real Vikings: Craftsmen, Traders, and Fearsome Raiders
Melvin Berger and Gilda Berger
National Geographic Society, 2003

Viking: The Norse Warrior's (Unofficial) Manual
John Haywood
Thames & Hudson, 2013

PLACES TO VISIT

L'Anse aux Meadows Viking Village
Newfoundland, Canada

The Jelling Stones
Jelling, Denmark

Jorvik Viking Centre
York, England

Trelleborg Viking Fortress
Trelleborg, Denmark

The Viking Ship Museum
Oslo, Norway

NG Staff for This Book
Shelby Alinsky, *Project Editor*
James Hiscott, Jr., *Art Director*
Lori Epstein, *Senior Photo Editor*
Carl Mehler, *Director of Maps*
Martin S. Walz, *Map Research and Production*
Paige Towler, *Editorial Assistant*
Sanjida Rashid and Rachel Kenny, *Design Production Assistants*
Colm McKeveny, *Rights Clearance Specialist*
Grace Hill, *Managing Editor*
Joan Gossett, *Senior Production Editor*
Lewis R. Bassford, *Production Manager*
Rachel Faulise, *Manager, Production Services*
Susan Borke, *Legal and Business Affairs*
Neal Edwards, *Imaging*

Published by the National Geographic Society
Gary E. Knell, *President and CEO*
John M. Fahey, *Chairman of the Board*
Melina Gerosa Bellows, *Chief Education Officer*
Declan Moore, *Chief Media Officer*
Hector Sierra, *Senior Vice President and General Manager,
    Book Division*

Senior Management Team, Kids Publishing and Media
Nancy Laties Feresten, *Senior Vice President*
Jennifer Emmett, *Vice President, Editorial Director, Kids Books*
Julie Vosburgh Agnone, *Vice President, Editorial Operations*
Rachel Buchholz, *Editor and Vice President,* NG Kids *magazine*
Michelle Sullivan, *Vice President, Kids Digital*
Eva Absher-Schantz, *Design Director*
Jay Sumner, *Photo Director*
Hannah August, *Marketing Director*
R. Gary Colbert, *Production Director*

Digital
Anne McCormack, *Director*
Laura Goetzel, Sara Zeglin, *Producers*
Emma Rigney, *Creative Producer*
Bianca Bowman, *Assistant Producer*
Natalie Jones, *Senior Product Manager*

**Editorial, Design, and Production by
    Plan B Book Packagers**

Captions
Cover: Norse literature tells of Viking warriors, or berserkers,
    looking fierce and wearing bear pelts in battle.
Page 1: A carved Viking head sits in a field.
Pages 2–3: Shetland Islanders set a replica Viking ship alight
    during the Up Helly Aa festival.

The National Geographic Society is one of the world's
largest nonprofit scientific and educational organizations.
Founded in 1888 to "increase and diffuse geographic
knowledge," the Society's mission is to inspire people to
care about the planet. It reaches more than 400 million
people worldwide each month through its official journal,
National Geographic, and other magazines; National
Geographic Channel; television documentaries; music;
radio; films; books; DVDs; maps; exhibitions; live events;
school publishing programs; interactive media; and
merchandise. National Geographic has funded more than
10,000 scientific research, conservation, and exploration
projects and supports an education program promoting
geographic literacy.

For more information, please visit
nationalgeographic.com, call 1-800-NGS LINE (647-5463),
or write to the following address:
National Geographic Society
1145 17th Street N.W.
Washington, D.C. 20036-4688 U.S.A.

Visit us online at nationalgeographic.com/books

For librarians and teachers: ngchildrensbooks.org

More for kids from National Geographic:
kids.nationalgeographic.com

For information about special discounts for bulk purchases,
please contact National Geographic Books Special Sales:
ngspecsales@ngs.org

For rights or permissions inquiries, please contact
National Geographic Books Subsidiary Rights:
ngbookrights@ngs.org

Paperback ISBN: 978-1-4263-2076-7
Reinforced library binding ISBN: 978-1-4263-2077-4

Printed in Hong Kong
15/THK/1